Original title:
Life's Not About the Destination, But the Detours

Copyright © 2025 Creative Arts Management OÜ
All rights reserved.

Author: Adeline Fairfax
ISBN HARDBACK: 978-1-80566-146-7
ISBN PAPERBACK: 978-1-80566-441-3

Winding Roads of Tomorrow

In a world where plans go astray,
I took a left when I should've stayed.
Wobbling wildly, I missed my mark,
But oh, what a show! Delightfully stark.

Unexpected Turns of the Heart

I'd mapped my route with utmost care,
Yet the coffee spill? A wild affair!
Across the street, a dog in a hat,
He barked at me, 'What's so wrong with that?'

Serendipity in Every Step

A stumble here, a giggle there,
Tripped on a cat, oh the flair!
Found a sandwich under my shoe,
Turns out it wasn't mine, not even a clue.

The Beauty of Uncharted Paths

So here's to the bumps on this road we ride,
To the goofy moments we cannot hide.
With a wink and a smile, let's take the call,
For the journey's the treasure, after all!

Curated Chaos

Plans laid out with great precision,
But fate delivers with indecision.
A coffee spill, a sudden detour,
Turns out I found a taco door!

Maps and guides, they bid me follow,
But squirrels play tricks, they're quite the scholars.
What once was straight, now twisty and wavy,
Is more like a story, amusing and crazy.

The Heart's Unscripted Route

I had a plan straight to the top,
Instead, I tripped on a donut shop.
With icing on my shirt and glee,
I danced in joy, wild and free.

Step by step, I lost my way,
But laughter found me every day.
Chasing dreams in mismatched shoes,
Each silly stumble, a joyful cruise.

Every Turn a Learning Curve

Maps in hand, I'm feeling bold,
Turn left, right, but wait, it's cold!
A detour leads to mischief found,
Skipping puddles, without a sound.

Turn after turn, I make a friend,
With jokes and coffee, the day won't end.
Each lesson taught with laughter's grace,
Who knew? A wrong turn's a happy place.

Embrace the Unforeseen

I took a ride on a whim, oh dear,
Ended up at a llama's sphere.
With furry friends, I laughed so bright,
Who needs a plan when this feels right?

The rain poured down, my shoes went squish,
But in the chaos, I found my wish.
Unplanned picnics and sunlit calls,
Every mishap, a comedy sprawls.

The Unexpected Beauty of Altered Routes

A wrong turn down a winding street,
Led to a taco truck, quite the treat.
We laughed at GPS's silly plight,
And danced beneath the neon light.

With signs that said 'Detour Ahead',
We found a park with a bench to spread.
A squirrel joined us for lunch that day,
It seemed to say, 'Come laugh and play!'

Footprints in Life's Mosaic

With every step on this twisted path,
We stumbled, we laughed, escaped the wrath.
A puddle splashed, our shoes now soaked,
Next came a mime, his silence provoked.

Through neighborhoods bright and alleys so grim,
We painted our story on a whimsical whim.
Footprints of joy mixed with mischief and mud,
Each detour a kaleidoscope, what a flood!

Chronicles of the Wandering Mind

Thoughts tripped over like a loose shoelace,
Snapping photos of clouds with a smiling face.
A coffee spill and a giggly squabble,
Each moment is gold, no need to hobble.

Bumps in the road, oh what a ride!
We chased the sunset, our eyes open wide.
Chirping the tunes of a wayward song,
In the end, it's all where we belong.

Adventures in Detour

A map that's wrong and yet so right,
Led us to a bakery, what a delight!
Cookies and laughter, we had our fill,
A detour made us laugh, what a thrill!

Speed bumps made us bounce in our seats,
Every twist, every turn, brought tasty treats.
A roadside attraction, a giant rubber duck,
In the end, who cares? We ran amok!

Moments on the Way

I took a left when I should have gone right,
And ended up in a pastry fight.
With cream-filled doughnuts in hand,
I declared victory, ruler of land!

A squirrel stole my sandwich with glee,
I chased it fast, shouting, "Come back to me!"
But it danced on a branch overhead,
I waved goodbye, let the squirrel be fed.

Unexpected Encounters on Familiar Paths

I met a llama at the coffee shop,
It wore a hat, said, "You really should stop!"
So I laughed and shared my drink,
Who knew llamas could offer such good advice to think?

A pigeon critiqued my outfit so bold,
"Those shoes went out with the last season's gold!"
I shrugged and grinned, who needs their approval?
The laughter we shared was quite the jewel.

The Splendor of Slightly Off-Course

I took a stroll near a twisty tree,
Only to find a dance-off, oh me!
Gnomes in garden hats were breaking it down,
While I joined in, wearing my best frown.

A detour led me to an impromptu fair,
With cotton candy clouds in the air.
I won a goldfish, named him Fred,
Life's little twists made my heart skip ahead.

Turning Points in the Ordinary

I decided to jog, just for a change,
But tripped on a curb—it seemed quite strange.
Landed in a garden of sunflowers tall,
They swayed in laughter, had a ball!

On a routine walk, I slipped on a shoe,
Found a turtle who shouted, "What's wrong with you?"
We giggled together, then made a pact,
To take the long path, that's an unwritten fact!

The Heart of Hidden Highways

In the midst of a shortcut, I missed my turn,
With GPS rebelling, my hopes did burn.
I found a gas station, with pie on display,
Turns out it was worth it, hooray for delay!

As I sipped on my soda, I met a strange cat,
He wore tiny glasses, and a big, chubby hat.
We spoke of existence and the price of a snack,
Who knew that detours meant meeting a chap?

Dodging potholes felt like an extreme sport,
With laughter and slip-ups, we held our own court.
Each bump on the road, a tale newly spun,
In the chaos of travel, I found loads of fun!

Finally reached my goal, but what did I find?
A parking lot full, and my peace of mind blind!
Yet in my wild trek, with flavors galore,
Those detours and stops made me love driving more!

Embracing the Thorns of the Journey

My plans laid out neatly, like socks in a drawer,
Then came a detour, I just couldn't ignore.
Turned left at the cactus, a sign of delight,
Prickly but funny, I chuckled at my plight.

The road less traveled, where llamas roam free,
They stared with confusion, perhaps judging me.
One gave me a wink, as if to say 'Hi!'
Now I'm questioning if I'm the silly guy.

Pulled into a diner with rainbow-frosted pie,
A waitress with sass asked me 'Do you fly?'
Between bursts of laughter, my worries took flight,
With each silly story, the mood felt just right.

So here's to the thorns that prickle our way,
They make for good tales that we love to replay.
Each twist and turn teaching us how to smile,
In this zany adventure, we wander each mile!

The Beauty of Minor Detours

I set out for coffee, quite a big dream,
But got lost in a shop selling ice cream.
Laughed as they scooped, my plans went astray,
With sprinkles and fudge, who needs the café?

A detour for nachos, I thought, why not?
Found myself at a flea market spot.
With trinkets and treasures that jumbled my brain,
Such wonders to see, who needs the train?

Enchanted Turns

With a map in my pocket, I took to the road,
 But soon I was lost, in laughter I glowed.
 Bunnies in hats had a dance-off with me,
 The GPS chuckled, 'Just let it be free!'

Around every corner, surprises would bloom,
 A pirate parade made my heart go vroom.
 Who knew that the way to the grocery store,
Would lead me to quests, leaving me wanting more?

Unfolding Stories from Side Roads

Once I was steady, my path was all planned,
Till I tripped on a rock and fell into sand.
An octopus waiter served cocktails on the beach,
He told me to stay; I thought of a screech!

A scooter appeared, I'm off to the race,
But it sputtered and coughed, oh what a disgrace!
The laughter erupted as I zigzagged and swerved,
Detours became tales that I really deserved.

The Curious Compass

The compass was spinning, where should I go?
I followed the chirps of a chicken in tow.
Through fields filled with daisies and crazy old trees,
I danced with the squirrels, oh what a tease!

My pizza was cold, but the stories were hot,
Found a treasure map in a pickled jar pot.
With every side street, the fun did grow fonder,
Embracing the chaos, oh what a blunder!

The Poetics of Pit Stops

In the midst of a drive, I took a wrong turn,
Found a quirky roadside, my stomach did yearn.
A diner named 'Sam's' with pies oh-so-sweet,
Left with a belly, and a smile, what a treat!

The GPS spoke, but I chose to stray,
Chasing cotton candy, and a bear that could play.
Each silly detour felt like a new chance,
To tango with strangers in a glorious dance.

Shades of Serendipity

The path ahead looked straight, tried to keep cool,
But stumbled on llamas at the town's petting pool.
In shades of surprise, I waved at the crowd,
Who knew such fun could be that loud?

Suddenly lost, I shrugged it away,
Danced with a squirrel who stole my croissant, hey!
A day full of laughter, not just a chore,
Found treasures of joy I had wanted more.

Between Here and There

Between my start and where I should be,
I stopped for a moment to glance at a tree.
A squirrel was chattering, giving a show,
I laughed so hard, almost lost my taco!

The road was a canvas, splashes of chance,
Every pit stop felt like a dance.
Missed my exit, but found a fair,
With cotton candy clouds, oh, what a scare!

Moments That Spark Change

Driving along with a plan in my mind,
A big ol' pothole had me realigned.
It pitched and it tossed, a comedic affair,
Landed in a festival, with balloons in the air!

Hiccups of fate, they brought me delight,
Met a juggler who dressed up as a knight.
What started as plans for a dull little quest,
Turned into stories that I love the best.

The Art of Getting Lost

In a maze of winding lanes,
With no map to my name,
I found a cow in pajamas,
Who said, 'This is my game!'

I tripped over a garden gnome,
Who winked and offered tea,
He claimed to talk to flowers,
And danced just like a bee.

Each turn a chance to chuckle,
With every twist and bend,
Missing signs for the highway,
But gaining laughs, my friend.

So next time you're unsure,
Just wander and embrace,
For every wrong direction,
May lead to joy's sweet face.

Moments Lurking in Shadows

Under a streetlamp's glow,
I met a cat in shoes,
He claimed to be a dancer,
And squeezed out all my blues.

The shadows whispered secrets,
Of treasures lost and found,
A squirrel held a banquet,
With acorns all around.

I stumbled on a pickle,
It rolled right past my toe,
In a race with a raccoon,
Who shouted, 'Go, go, go!'

So when the night gets silly,
And laughter's in the air,
Embrace the smoky whispers,
And dance without a care.

Stardust from Side Streets

Down an alley paved with dreams,
I bumped into a star,
He wore a shiny tutu,
And claimed he'd traveled far.

Around the block, some jellybeans,
Were dancing on the ground,
I joined their sweet parade,
And spun round, round, round!

A ladybug in sunglasses,
Charmed everyone in line,
She said, 'Join the conga,
We're having quite a time!'

So if you roam those side streets,
And feel too shy to twirl,
Just know that twinkling wonders,
Can brighten up your world.

Curves and Corners of Existence

In a car packed with old dreams,
We drove without a care,
Finding curves and corners,
Like treasure hidden where!

A llama crossed the highway,
Wearing a party hat,
She shouted, 'Stop the engine!
Let's do the 'Llama Chat!'

With every turn we giggled,
At signs that lost their way,
A detour to the cookie shop,
Is how we spent our day.

So swerve a little wider,
Make memories to last,
For every twist and tangle,
Brings joy that's unsurpassed.

Unplanned Adventures Await

When plans go sideways, grab your gear,
The unexpected brings the best cheer.
Lost in the woods, but what a sight,
A squirrel on a skateboard gives pure delight.

Turn left instead of right, oh dear,
Just follow the sound of that loud cheer.
Who knew this road led to ice cream fun,
As we race with seagulls under the sun?

A wrong turn means selfies galore,
With goats in sunglasses—you can't ignore.
Laughing as we trip on a garden gnome,
These wacky moments feel like home.

So when the route gets quite askew,
Embrace the chaos, let joy ensue.
With unplanned adventures at our feet,
Each twist and turn is a comic feat.

Curves in the Journey

A winding road, the GPS screams,
But who needs maps when you're living dreams?
We zigzag through towns we can't pronounce,
With snacks from roadside stands that we renounce.

Each curve reveals a brand new face,
A llama in sunglasses wins the race.
We sip lemonade in a bizarre town square,
And dance with the locals with nary a care.

The way is bumpy, full of surprise,
A donut shop's glow meets our hungry eyes.
With every pothole, laughter rings loud,
We're just a silly, detour-loving crowd.

So let's embrace the goofy and weird,
In winding paths, our spirits are steered.
Curves, oh curves, lead us astray,
But every misstep brightens our day.

Finding Beauty in the Bumps

Bumpy roads make for stories grand,
Like the time we slipped in ice cream land.
With every jolt and surprising shake,
We've got tales to tell and laughs to make.

A pothole hid a treasure map,
Spilled soda turned into a funny slap.
With every bump, our hearts take flight,
Finding joy in chaos feels so right.

Stumbling on sidewalks and missing a beat,
We dance like no one and feel the heat.
Each tumble and trip becomes a song,
In this clumsy adventure, we all belong.

So when the path feels rough and grim,
Just giggle and sing your own silly hymn.
Embrace the bumps, the crazy ride,
For in these moments, we truly thrive.

Serendipity on the Trail

Oh look, a river where there shouldn't be,
We'll paddle a kayak and splash with glee.
Serendipity whispers, let's take a break,
How did we end up at this giant cake?

We stumble upon a parade of cats,
Wearing tiny hats, oh imagine that!
With laughter that echoes through the trees,
Who knew detours could bring us such ease?

A hidden café serves the weirdest brew,
With flavors so strange, who would've knew?
Each sip ignites a chuckle and grin,
Serendipity leads us, let the fun begin!

So journey along, unfurl your map,
Explore every nook, every lovely flap.
In forked paths and turns, joy fills the air,
For life's sweet surprises are waiting there.

Between Plan A and B

I packed my bags with dreams galore,
But ended up at a llama store.
My GPS led me far off track,
Now I'm the king of a llama pack.

I planned to eat at a fancy place,
But found a taco truck in a race.
With mustard on my cheek, I smile wide,
Who knew tacos would be my pride?

I thought of sunsets, romantic and bright,
But got caught in a feud with a kite.
Chasing it down, I lost my hat,
Caught by a dog that was more than fat.

So here's the twist that proved to be fun,
The best times come when plans come undone.
Llamas and tacos are where it's at,
Make a new plan? Nah, I'll pet that cat!

Start with a Step, End with a Story

I took a step, oh what a sight,
And landed right into a pie fight.
With blueberry splatters all on my face,
I couldn't help but laugh in that sticky place.

Thought I'd jog, felt quite elite,
But stumbled over my own two feet.
I rolled like a burrito off the trail,
And ended up in a barn with a snail.

I peered ahead for a glorious view,
But tripped on a root and fell flat too.
A squirrel sat laughing from his nearby tree,
As I declared, 'This must be my destiny!'

So next time you plan a cakewalk stroll,
Embrace each detour, rock and roll.
The stories you'll have will sweetly unfold,
With laughter and joy worth more than gold!

Somewhere Between Destination and Divagation

I set my sights on a far-off town,
But somehow ended up in a clowning gown.
The GPS said right, but I went left,
Now I'm a performer and quite bereft.

I tried to find the famous café,
But found a chicken that wanted to play.
It danced on my feet, I nearly screamed,
With feathers flying, I felt so redeemed.

Onward! I marched to a festival bright,
Only to realize it's a pillow fight.
With feathers in my hair and a smile so wide,
It's a bumpy ride that I can't abide.

Between all the turns that led me astray,
I found hidden glories along the way.
With jesters and pillows, I danced with glee,
In this funny journey, I found me!

The Trail Beneath Our Feet

I planned to hike a mountain tall,
But tripped on a rock and took a fall.
Rolling down, I landed in mud,
Now I'm a walking, talking chocolate bud.

The nature I sought was elusive and sly,
Yet friends joined in to wonder why.
With sticks in hand and laughter unbound,
We made a party on this muddy ground.

A squirrel named Frank joined our crew,
With a plan to raid our lunch, so true.
Picnic spread out, he aimed for the bread,
But we all just laughed, and then we fled.

So here's the lesson from our messy quest,
Sometimes the tangles create the best fest.
With mud on our boots and laughter galore,
It's the trails, not the peaks, we adore!

Curves and Crossroads

I took a left when I should've turned right,
Ended up lost in a karaoke night.
Singing off-key with a wig on my head,
The map in my pocket, I decided to shred.

Road signs flashing, I went for a spin,
Chasing a raccoon, I thought it a win.
Turns out it led to a pie-eating contest,
I took home a trophy, I must confess.

Hit a pothole and splashed in the lake,
Just when I thought I'd catch a big wake.
Boat fishing turned to a gourmet delight,
Fish tacos served up, it was quite the sight.

So here I am at this crossroad of fun,
Where plans went awry but joy had begun.
I'll take more detours, I'm ready to roam,
With laughter as fuel, I'm always at home.

Treasure Maps of Experience

Lost with my map and a quest for some gold,
Found a cat with a monocle, brazen and bold.
He led me to tacos, not treasure divine,
But a salsa so spicy, it sure felt like crime.

Can't locate the X where the riches do lie,
But I found some new friends, oh me, oh my!
We danced like sardines, our rhythm was so blurred,
In search of the good times, I've never deterred.

The compass spinning wild, oh what a mess,
My GPS just said 'Nope!'—what a distress!
So we followed the smell of a pizza delight,
And feasted till dawn under stars shining bright.

With each twist and turn, life's map intertwines,
The journey, it seems, is worth all the signs.
For who needs a fortune when laughter is free?
Embracing the chaos, just let it be me!

Carefully Crafted Chaos

Planned my route with precision so neat,
But the ice cream truck called, how could I retreat?
Detours of flavor, oh sweet, sweet regret,
Turns out I've a tummy I can't quite forget.

Oh look, there's a squirrel in a tiny red car,
He waved as he zoomed, it's a nutty bazaar.
Caught in the traffic of giggles and glee,
I lost sight of order, and savored the spree.

Ordered a smoothie, but got a milkshake,
Sipped it so fast, made a mess to partake.
I laughed at the chaos that blessed my whole day,
In the land of the silly, I'm here to stay.

A corkscrew of mishaps, I twist and I turn,
Finding joy in the jumbles, there's much to learn.
When plans go awry, I just grin and embrace,
For life's greatest moments are found in this space.

Fleeting Whispers of the Road

Pulled over for gas, I bumped into fate,
A llama in sunglasses, now that's first rate.
He sipped on a soda, laid back like a pro,
I joined him in laughter, sharing stories to flow.

With each blurry mile, adventures unfurled,
Found a village of gnomes, a whimsical world.
They taught me to dance upon mushrooms so round,
In the midst of detours, pure joy I had found.

Got sidetracked once more by a rainbow parade,
Floats made of candy, oh what a charade!
I twirled and I laughed, ketchup for confetti,
In this lively circus, my spirit feels ready.

So take in the whispers, the sights, the delight,
For the road may be winding, but oh, what a sight!
Embrace every bump, every turn that feels wrong,
In the chaos, the laughter, is where we belong.

Marvels in the Margins

On a trip to see the sights,
We took a wrong turn, oh what a fright!
Ended up in a little café,
Where the pie was cheap and the laughs were gay.

We missed the tour and took a stroll,
Found a duck that stole my roll!
With each misstep, a story to tell,
Who knew that detours could go so well?

Maps in hand, we chart our course,
But detours lead to hidden resource!
Lost in a field, we danced with bees,
Who knew blooming flowers would bring such glee?

So here we are, with smiles so wide,
Embracing all mishaps, we take in stride.
For every wrong turn and twist and bend,
Is just another way to find a friend.

Heartbeats on Unfamiliar Roads

Driving down roads we've never seen,
With snacks galore—we're quite the team!
A sign that reads "bizarre museum,"
Let's check it out, what could be the harm?

Inside there hung a giant shoe,
We couldn't stop laughing, what a view!
To think we almost drove on by,
Now it's a memory that will never die!

Every red light turned into a joke,
As we made faces, giggling till we spoke.
"Why did the chicken cross?" I asked with glee,
"To confuse the driver, just like we!"

On this wild ride, no hour is dull,
With every bump, my heart feels full.
So here's to the roads that lead us astray,
A playlist of laughter—what a fine day!

Unwritten Pages of Our Travels

With blank pages in a brand-new book,
We set out to explore, take a look.
But coffee spills and muddy shoes,
Made our stories—oh what a ruse!

"Look at that tree! It's totally misshaped!"
We laughed so hard, the fun we draped.
Who needs a guide when we have delight,
In trees that resemble our wild nights?

Each detour unveils a new charade,
Like ordering sushi that tastes like jade.
Finding treasure where none was sought,
True joy was forged in the chaos we caught.

So here we scribble as the roads unfurl,
Adventure unleashed, it's a funny swirl!
We gather tales where we misstep wide,
In every mishap, we wear pride!

The Adventure Beyond the Horizon

Over the hills, we march towards fun,
Only to find it's begun to run.
Off track, we chortle as cows stare back,
And one mooed loud, "You're off the track!"

With no GPS to keep us constrained,
We chase rainbows over fields untrained.
A leap into puddles, shoes full of squelch,
With every splash, our giggles welch.

"Do you smell that?" a food stand calls,
Their "world-famous" fries break down the walls.
Of plans laid out, we say, "Never mind!"
In every snack, a memory we find.

So let us journey where feet may stray,
With no expectations to lead the way.
In every detour, mischief will sprout,
It's the crazy moments that life's all about!

Footpaths of Fate

Stumbling down a winding road,
I trip on every stone I've strode.
With laughter loud and worries small,
I take missteps, hear fate's call.

A squirrel steals my sandwich too,
I chase it fast, oh what a view!
The grassy knoll, it steals my shoe,
And now I hop, a sight so true!

Through twists and turns, I lose my way,
Yet every wrong's a chance to play.
With silly signs and quirky sights,
I find joy in those funny flights.

So here I wander, full of cheer,
With every laugh, I shed my fear.
Embrace the bends, let chaos reign,
For in the mess, we break the chain.

Journeys of Discovery

Took a left when I should've turned right,
Now I'm lost in the pizza night.
With cheese in hand, I make a friend,
A tourist who plans to loose, not mend.

We find a map that's upside down,
Two clowns in a misplaced town.
With giggles loud, we roam the street,
In the great escape, we find our beat.

A fountain's splash brings spark and glee,
I splash the stranger next to me.
His frown turns to a laughing shout,
Together, we goof without a doubt.

So here's to paths that veer and sway,
With every misstep, let's dance away.
In every twist, a chance to dream,
Adventure hides in every scheme.

The Shape of the Unseen

In shadows where the lost things roam,
I spy a cat that calls me 'home'.
With whiskers twitching, it gives a glance,
And I'm off in a furry dance.

Around the corner, I spot a tree,
Its branches wave and beckon me.
I climb like a clown, oh what a mess,
Then tumble down in my best dress!

With giggles shared and laughter bright,
My heart ignites with every slight.
For hidden shapes create the fun,
Unseen gems, oh how we run!

So let us lose the mapped out path,
Instead, let giggles lead our math.
In every tumble, joy is gleaned,
In the unseen, our hearts convened.

Transformations in Transit

On buses filled with vibrant folks,
We share our tales, we share our jokes.
A dance-off breaks between the seats,
As strangers turn to funky beats.

My coffee spills, a splash of brown,
A moment's chaos, joy's renown.
With laughter shared, I meet new sights,
In these small trips, our friendship lights.

From park to street, we twist and glide,
Transformed by every silly ride.
A flying hat, a lost umbrella,
In transit's charm, I meet a fella.

So let the journey take a spin,
For in the chaos, we begin.
With laughter loud and memories grand,
The fun awaits, let's make a stand!

Serene Skids and Joyful Jars

In a car that wobbles, we take a turn,
Missed the exit? Oh well, we learn!
A jar of snacks spills, popcorn flies,
Laughter erupts, oh how time flies!

GPS laughs, recalculates with glee,
Every wrong turn brings more laughs, you see?
We spot a llama wearing a hat,
And capture the moment, imagine that!

Chasing sunsets on a one-lane road,
Fun found where the wild weeds grow.
Flat tires and detours, it's all a riot,
Every twist and turn, we quietly try it!

So here's to the flaws, oh what a ride!
The map's just a guide, let joy be our stride.
With serenity in skids and joy in jars,
We embrace the chaos, reach for the stars!

Shadows and Silhouettes of the Journey

As shadows chime, we dance in the light,
Missed the path? That's alright!
Silhouettes of laughter, we strike a pose,
The journey's much better than a map that knows!

We wander through fields of silly sight,
A misplaced umbrella makes everyone bright.
With each clumsy step, we trip and we fall,
But giggles arise, we bounce from it all!

The sign says 'stop,' but we go on ahead,
In a world of detours, we laugh instead.
With every misstep, our hearts take flight,
Shadows tell tales of a wild delight!

So here we progress in whimsical ways,
Turning dull moments into vibrant plays.
In the silhouettes of our frolic and fun,
The journey's our treasure, we're never quite done!

Hues of a Happy Accident

Colors collide as we take a wrong street,
A happy accident, how sweet a treat!
Splash of blue from a spilled soda shade,
Turns the ordinary into a vibrant parade!

With each squinted glance and dodgy turn,
We find hidden joys just waiting to burn.
Red lights and green lights make quite the show,
As we dance in the traffic, all aglow!

The map has a mind, but we choose to play,
Tracing our future in a colorful way.
Every bump and bruise sprinkles glittering vibes,
In hues of joy, our true joy thrives!

So let's paint this journey in bright strokes today,
With laughter as pigment, we'll find a new way.
Through happy accidents, our hearts shall expand,
In the gallery of travels, together we stand!

Explorations in the Unplanned

Diving into chaos without a clue,
A wrong turn leads us to a breathtaking view.
Clumsy adventures and pie in the face,
Each twist and each detour adds to our grace!

As umbrellas open in blustery wind,
We sail like ships, adventure has sinned!
Bump into a party, crash with a cheer,
'Unplanned' is the way we conquer our fear!

Maps are for those who fear to explore,
We let serendipity open the door.
In this dance of wobbles, we joyfully prance,
With goofy grins as our ultimate stance!

So join the parade of the unplanned, my friend,
Where every faux pas is a joy to extend.
Through explorations and laughter we glide,
In this grand old adventure, we joyously ride!

Making Memories Off the Beaten Track

We took a wrong turn near the old oak tree,
Ended up at a llama farm, who knew, not me.
They laughed as we fed them our lunch to share,
Who knew, in mischief, we'd find our flair?

A pit stop by puddles, we splashed and we slid,
A detour declared, like mischievous kids.
Instead of the timeline we thought we would trace,
We danced in the rain, wild smiles on our face.

Our map was a joke, with squiggles and lines,
But every wrong turn was better than finds.
For laughter and joy, so silly yet grand,
How blissful it felt to be lost, hand in hand.

Journeys We Never Planned

On Tuesday we planned to visit the coast,
But a flat tire became our unwelcome host.
We ended up jamming at a roadside stand,
With a banjo and laughter, an unforgettable band.

A kitchen in chaos, everyone cooks,
Turning bland sandwiches into fancy looks.
With every mishap, our spirits just soared,
We cheered every fumble and deeply adored.

Our eyes filled with wonders we never had sought,
Remember those detours, they'd never be fought.
For this unplanned journey, with joy thick as glue,
Gave stories of laughter, to share anew.

Embracing the Unforeseen

A signpost that quirked, it said 'Follow Me!'
Led us to ice cream, oh, what a spree!
For every wrong street we calling divine,
We'd prove one scoop leads to extra, not fine.

A mishap in parking, our van goes astray,
Till we stumbled on dancers in colorful sway.
With each twist and turn, a giggling increase,
We rolled in the grass, we found our release.

The touristy spots, they'll have to wait,
We're sipping our drinks, discussing our fate.
With songs and adventures we never did foresee,
It's the moments unplanned that forever will be.

Echoes of a Meandering Mind

A compass on strike and the GPS down,
We end up in fields where cows wear a crown.
Their mooing in rhythm, a show of delight,
We danced with the dairy in soft morning light.

With sandwiches flying, we lost all our pride,
A chase for lost crumbs became a wild ride.
The map was a puzzle, confoundingly fun,
We veered off the trail but found the bright sun.

Through highways and byways, in laughter we roamed,
Each blunder became the pride of our home.
Not the plan that we drew, but the moments so bright,
Echoes of joy, our mishaps igniting delight.

Dance of the Diversions

I took a right where I should've gone left,
Found a goat with a top hat, such a theft!
We twirled and we spun, what a sight to behold,
In the chaos of laughter, my heart turned to gold.

The street sign wobbled like a drunken friend,
Pointing to nowhere, or maybe the end,
Each bend in the road was a giggle and cheer,
With a hiccuping car that just refused to steer.

With each joyful turn, I lost track of time,
Chasing the sunset, it felt like a rhyme.
Who cares 'bout destinations, I'm loving this spree,
Dancing through diversions, so wild and so free!

Finding Bliss in the Byways

Stumbled upon ice cream, a happy surprise,
Sundae in hand, oh, how my heart flies!
But wait, there's a llama, wearing shoes oh so bright,
In a world full of chaos, it felt so right.

The GPS shouted, 'Turn left, turn right!'
But I was too busy with a balloon fight.
Giggles erupted from kids in the park,
Their laughter, a symphony that lit up the dark.

Each twist was a treasure, each wrong was a laugh,
Finding these moments felt like a craft.
So here are my maps, I'll gladly misread,
For bliss in the byways fulfills every need!

Treasures in the Unplanned

I aimed for the beach, ended up with a cat,
Who purred and meowed, just like a diplomat.
She led me to wonders I never would seek,
Through alleys of nonsense, the funny and sleek.

Trip over a taco truck, what a fun fate,
With each cheesy bite, I was feeling so great.
The map's in my pocket, but that's just for show,
'Cause unplanned adventures are always a go!

Like finding a dance in a puddle of rain,
Kicking up joy, I forget all my pain.
Oh, treasures surround me, wherever I roam,
In the heart of the funny, I've found my true home.

Memories Wrapped in Wander

Packed my bags, but forgot my keys,
Stood in the doorway, just chuckling with ease.
Who needs a plan when you've got a good laugh?
I'll hitch a ride on a quirky giraffe!

Sipped coffee with pigeons, they joked and they cooed,
'More muffins!' they squawked, they were quite the brood.
With each silly moment, my worries just fade,
In this dance of distraction, my heart is remade.

Through chaos and whimsy, my spirit sets free,
Memories wrapped in wander, come dance along with me!

Let's savor the mischief, the fun in the ride,
In laughter and joy, I'll always abide.

Paths Less Traveled

I took a left where I should've gone right,
Found a café with muffins, what a delight!
The GPS recalibrated with a sigh,
While I munched on sweets, oh my, oh my!

I met a cat who fancied a chat,
And a squirrel voiced strong opinions on fat.
We debated politics over tea,
Turns out, the joke's on me, oh glee!

The road was bumpy, the trip felt long,
But those silly moments sang the sweetest song.
I skipped a meeting for a dance in the rain,
And laughed at the chaos while waiting for my train.

Every twist and turn put a smile on my face,
Dancing with strangers at an unplanned place.
Pathways may wander, but joy stays in sight,
In the end, it's the journey that feels just right.

Whispers of the Wandering Heart

I packed a bag, forgot my phone,
Rode a bike, and felt like a drone.
A dog chased me down for a play,
And off the main road, I lost my way!

Stumbling on a festival, what a sight!
Twirling with strangers, lost track of the night.
I joked with a mime, no words were shared,
Yet laughter's the language, we both declared!

In a town named after a fruit, how grand!
Sampled jams, played in the band.
The detours offered more than I could expect,
With each silly setback, new joys intersected.

The whispers of paths where the maps grow dim,
Paint stories of detours, no need to swim.
So I toast to the moments that life spins around,
With friends made in chaos, love knows no bounds!

Open Roads and Open Minds

With windows down, the tunes on blast,
I took a wrong turn but had a blast.
Found a sign that said, "World's Biggest Pie!"
Left my worries, gave a carefree sigh.

The GPS was wrong, I was just bemused,
Found a quirky shop, and came so amused.
A garden gnome told me to stay for a while,
In this detoured adventure, I found my style.

Each mile I drove brought wacky delight,
A truck stop karaoke? What a night!
Sang off-key, but who really cares?
In this mad joyful ride, my spirit flares!

So raise a cup to the roads we don't plan,
Where laughter and quirks go hand in hand.
Open hearts lead to fun far and wide,
In the wanderlust dance, we take it in stride.

Treads on Unmarked Ground

I tripped on a curb, fell right to the street,
Met some friendly pigeons, oh how they greet!
They coo-ed their wisdom; I honked like a goose,
Laughter erupted; I felt like a moose.

Found a trail where the flowers gossip,
With colors that pop, they'll never stop.
A rabbit in shades taught me how to groove,
As we danced to the tunes of nature's smooth move.

Driving past fields, the cows gave me looks,
"Is that a human or writing a book?"
They gathered around, I shared my grand tales,
Of travels and snacks, and wild dreams that sail.

So here's to the paths that aren't on the charts,
Where fun and folly sing at their parts.
In the dance of the random, we find our ground,
Treading softly where laughter is found.

Journeys Over Destinations

Pack your bags, but hold your snacks,
For all the plans are just abstract.
The map says straight, but we took a side,
Chasing chubby squirrels with glee and pride.

Who knew the donut shop was a shrine?
With sprinkles galore, we lost track of time.
Each bite a detour, a curve in the road,
Turns out, calories have no zip code!

We took a left when we meant to go right,
Now we're lost in a maze – what a sight!
But laughter echoes through every twist,
Even our GPS gives up in the mist.

So here's to the bumps where the fun begins,
Where the detours bring laughter, not just grins.
With each wrong turn, we find something new,
Journeys over goals, that's the best view!

Stumbling Upon Wonder

Oh boy, a flat tire at mile one-oh-one,
We're stuck here, but hey, let's have some fun!
A picnic on grass with ants as our guests,
Where treasure and trouble come dressed as jest.

The sign says 'closed' but the door's ajar,
We wander in, it's a quirky bazaar.
With odd hats and socks that don't match,
We giggle and dance in a vintage mismatch!

Chasing rainbows that lead to ice cream,
A scoop, then two, it's a glorious dream.
Who cares about time? We're happy and free,
The best kind of wonder is found at a spree.

So stumble with joy, let adventure unfold,
Each twist and each turn is more precious than gold.
In the mess and the mishaps, pure magic we find,
Stumbling upon wonder, let's not be confined!

Footprints in the Unknown

With boots on my feet and a snack in tow,
I wander the paths where the wildflowers grow.
Each step I take feels like a dance,
In this upside-down waltz of happenstance.

Found a llama wearing funny shades,
Who knew they could be such stylish blades?
We giggled and posed, took a snapshot quick,
This detour turned out to be quite the trick!

Washing my hands at a fountain so grand,
It turned into a splash fight, oh wasn't it planned?
We left some footprints and a whole lot of cheer,
In the book of detours, we'll hold these dear.

So let's wander on paths that don't have a map,
With each silly moment, we fall in a flap.
Footprints of laughter in places unknown,
In the heart of the journey, true joy is sown!

Mosaic of Meandering Moments

In a car full of snacks, we hit the road,
Where misfits gather, our wild stories flowed.
With a GPS that's in vacation mode,
We chuckled at paths that we almost stowed.

A roadside stand with the world's weirdest fruit,
We dared each other to take a big bite, cute!
Mangoes that jiggle, bananas that sing,
What a unexpected little fun thing!

Lost in a town where the traffic lights shine,
Saw an old man juggling, what a sign!
We stopped for a show, and oh, what a blast,
In our scrapbook of life, we found memories vast.

Mosaic of moments, some silly, some sweet,
With each quirky turn, our laughter complete.
So here's to the path that bends every day,
In the art of meandering, the fun's here to stay!

Echoes of the Wandering Spirit

In a quest for the best pie,
I took a wrong turn, oh my!
The GPS laughed with glee,
As I found a yard sale knee-deep in tea.

Each twist and each bend,
Led to friendships that blend.
Lost in the maze of delight,
I found a cat who claimed the night.

Maps are just scribbles in sand,
While the journey takes a wacky stand.
Through wild hills and funny towns,
I collected more smiles than crowns.

So here's to the trips that go wrong,
Where laughter and memories belong.
With a suitcase of quirks we embrace,
The detours bring joy to our race.

Stories in the Stumbles

I tripped over shoes left behind,
In a race with the silly wind so unkind.
Laughter echoed in the park,
As I gained a new spark in the dark.

A fallen branch turned into a throne,
Where I ruled my kingdom of groans.
The squirrels threw acorns, their cheers,
As I danced to shake off my fears.

With every side step and misstep so bold,
There's poetry waiting to be told.
The tales of the paths I did trod,
Are seedbeds where true joy is prod.

Stumbling is just part of the ride,
With laughter our trusty guide.
We'll paint the world with absurd flair,
As we wander, we'll always share.

Pathways of Possibility

I sought a straight path, neat and clear,
But found a pancake house, oh dear!
With syrup rivers flowing wide,
I took a detour, and what a ride!

Some paths led me to quirky cafes,
With foghorns blaring in funny ways.
A dog in a hat gave me a wink,
As I savored my coffee, I dared to think.

Adventure hid in the wrong turn's embrace,
Where every bump felt like grace.
With chalk drawings made by local rascals,
My worries dissolved like fine pastels.

I danced with the leaves in the breeze,
And forgot all about my keys.
Embracing the humor in every twist,
A wild path is one not to miss.

Journeys that Define Us

With a suitcase bursting with whims,
I set off where the wild croon hymns.
I missed the bus, ended up in a zoo,
Where llamas thought I was coming for stew!

Paths go sideways without a fright,
As clown shoes dancing steal the night.
A pie-eating contest danced on my route,
I joined in, no shame, shouting, "Let's scoot!"

Every bump painted a hilarious tale,
With mayhem and laughter as my sail.
We'll find ourselves in the wild shuffle,
The beauty is found in the joyful scuffle.

So cheers to the twists we embrace,
Where smiles hide in every space.
Each stumble and folly we'll cherish and trust,
In this crazy ride, it's hope that we lust.

Detours of the Soul

When the GPS went mad, I grinned,
Took a right where I should've skimmed.
Saw a llama in a pink tutu,
Wonders round every corner, who knew?

Traffic cones dancing, what a sight,
A squirrel on roller skates, pure delight.
Chasing snacks as I lost my way,
Wherever I wander, it's a cabaret.

People laugh at my map in hand,
But I found a circus in candyland.
Twists and turns, with giggles bright,
Every wrong turn felt so right.

I'll keep my eyes peeled for the strange,
No path can bind me, I'll always change.
In laughter-filled streets, I claim my roll,
Joy's the secret on detours of the soul.

The Space Between Steps

I tripped on a curb, oh what a clatter,
A dog in a bowtie stopped to chatter.
My shoelace danced like it had a role,
Each moment whispers in the space between steps, oh soul!

Skipping puddles felt like a game,
The ducks quacked loudly; they knew my name.
Every sidestep turned into a jump,
Wit and whimsy, my cheerleader's hunch.

A friendly cat offered sage advice,
'Life's a buffet, but be sure to slice!'
I laughed and snorted as I hopped on through,
Sprinting from troubles, like a zany zoo.

There's joy in the stumble, joy in the sway,
Each shuffled step makes a funny display.
With every misstep, my heart's on a roll,
Finding my rhythm, in the space of my stroll.

Revelations in the Rearview

As I gazed back, what came into view,
A parade of mishaps, a hullabaloo.
A cow wearing shades, what was the deal?
Laughter echoing, it's hard to conceal.

Just past the corner, a dance-off broke out,
Two mice in tuxedos, shaking without doubt.
A hiccup in time, as funny as pie,
Revelations in the rearview make me sigh.

Chasing tires rolled off the beaten track,
A sandwich with legs began to attack.
In twists and turns, I caught the surprise,
Life's antic-filled journey, a feast for the eyes.

In reflection, I find what brings me cheer,
With chuckles and giggles, I hold them dear.
Every blunder's a treasure, a story to weave,
In the rearview mirror, it's hard to believe.

Glimpses of Grace on Side Streets

Down cobblestone paths where the wildflowers grow,
I encountered a mime that stole quite the show.
His gestures so grand, they lit up the lane,
While I tried to guess if he felt any strain.

Past coffee shops brewing rumors and banter,
A cat with a top hat joined the canter.
Each side street offered a quirky parade,
Glimpses of grace on this whimsical glide.

With laughter like confetti, the world spins around,
In alleys and corners where stardust is found.
Mismatched socks danced, and the night felt young,
In every detour, a song's worth was sung.

I'll wander the world, with a grin on my face,
Chasing oddities, each charming embrace.
Wherever I stroll, and however I roam,
It's the quirks on side streets that bring me home.

The Sweetness of Tangential Paths

When GPS said, 'Turn right now,'
I thought I'd take the scenic route somehow.
A donut shop caught my hungry gaze,
I parked for hours, lost in a glaze.

With every wrong turn, I found a delight,
A street performer dancing, oh what a sight!
Life's surprises, they wrap like a gift,
Who knew a detour could offer such lift?

So here's to the bends that veer off the track,
Where laughter and joy have no need to lack.
Forget the straight paths that lead to the goal,
For joy in the journey revives the soul.

Take a snack break, skip a turn or two,
Embrace the twists that are quirky and new.
For each silly sidestep brings stories galore,
Let's wander the world and discover much more!

Whispers from the Wilderness

Amidst the trees, a squirrel did call,
It shouted, 'Hey, come see this fall!'
I followed the sound, tripped over a root,
Landed face-first in a pile of cute.

Nature threw me a pie in the face,
Laughter erupted—what a silly place!
The trails were fuzzy, but don't you fret,
Each step was a giggle I'll never forget.

So heed not the signs, let whims take the lead,
Adventure awaits, just follow the seed.
A winding path may not follow the map,
But what's lost is found in a cozy mishap.

The sound of the wild, it dances and spins,
With laughter as balm, and mischief begins.
So let's wander far, let our hearts be wild,
For weird little paths make us nature's child!

In the Footsteps of Chance

Once I set out, quite sure of my plan,
To grab a cold drink in a green can.
But fate tricked me, I made a wrong choice,
Ended up dancing with a chicken's voice.

Along the way, I stumbled on art,
A lady with socks, now that's a fine start!
Her crazy creations were bright as can be,
I left with a hat, and a chuckle, you see.

Never too late for a twist in the tale,
With chance as my map, I set sail.
In giggles and gags, I found my own way,
Carefree and happy, come what may.

So if your compass feels lost in the fray,
Trust that those moments will brighten your day.
Each stumble, each slip, is just part of the dance,
So leap with a laugh, and embrace every chance!

Boundless Journeys Beyond Maps

With a map in my pocket and snacks on the side,
I ventured to places where surprises hide.
But bad directions took me far from the plot,
Found a taco truck instead, which hit the spot.

While trying to find that old fountain's chill,
I discovered a band, their music was thrill.
Boogied and swayed, forgot where I'd go,
Losing myself in the rhythm's flow.

Maps may confine, like rules in a game,
But twisty adventures are never the same.
With laughter as fuel, and fun in the spark,
Each quirky sidetrack lights up the dark.

So wander a little, let spontaneity reign,
In chuckles and frolics, you'll find joy again.
For every detour that takes you askew,
Brings stories to tell, and laughter anew!

The Magic Found in Meanderings

Wandering through the garden of glee,
Tripping over weeds, oh dear me!
A squirrel steals my sandwich, quite rude,
Yet laughter fills the air, it's all good.

I take a wrong turn, end up at a fair,
Eating cotton candy, without a care.
The map says go straight, I say, 'Not today!'
Adventure calls louder than plans made in clay.

Lost in a maze of delightful quirks,
Chasing butterflies, avoiding the jerks.
I find a treasure of laughter and cheer,
In twists and turns, I shed every fear.

So here's to the paths that twist and shout,
To the wrong ways that turn into a route.
For every misstep, a dance to behold,
In the magic of meandering, life unfolds.

Bright Spots on the Map of Discovery

I set out to conquer the straight and the true,
But bumped into a llama, what's it to do?
We shared a snack, I named him Lou,
He taught me to dance and how to chew.

With directions that led me astray,
I found a spot where the bluebirds play.
An ice cream truck, oh what a sight!
I said, 'Forget the goal, let's have a bite.'

Maps with X's marked where I should go,
But zigging and zagging brought more glow.
Each bright spot shining as I roam,
Every detour comes with ice cream cones.

Discovery is sweet, just like a summer's day,
For in every misstep, there's fun on display.
I'll dance with Lou as the sun sinks low,
And treasure each moment, just letting it flow.

Pathways of the Heart

With a compass that spins in circles, I roam,
My heart is the guide, it feels like home.
Through alleys of laughter, I skip, I sing,
With each little bump, I find my spring.

Stray dogs join me on this joyous spree,
They bark at the wind, oh so carefree.
We dodge all the puddles and dance through the rain,
In the pathways of heart, there's no need for pain.

Unexpected turns bring out the best,
Like finding a napkin that's now a treasure chest.
Each twist in my journey means another fun tale,
Like riding a turtle and sailing a whale.

So let us wander without any cares,
The paths of the heart lead to joyous flares.
With laughter as fuel and fun as the art,
We'll enjoy every moment, that's the clever part.

Tangles in the Tapestry of Time

Knots in my shoelaces, oh what a chore,
A tumble and stumble, but I laugh even more.
Each misadventure a stitch in my quilt,
Woven with giggles, not a trace of guilt.

Skipping through time like a rock in a brook,
The pages of moments in every nook.
I found an old hat that belonged to a cat,
He winked as he danced, imagine that chat!

Mistakes turn to stories with each reroute,
Like baking a pie that comes out as a brout.
Yet flavors of laughter sprinkle my dish,
In the tangles of time, I find every wish.

So here's to the detours, the twists and spins,
To the laughter that blossoms and never thins.
In the tapestry tangled, I weave where I roam,
Finding joy in the journey, forever my home.

The Joy of Getting Lost

Wandered off the beaten track,
With GPS on a snack break.
Turned left instead of right,
Oh look! A squirrel in flight.

Found a café up a tree,
Served tea with a side of glee.
Met a cat that played guitar,
Said we're lost, but what a star!

The road ahead is but a tease,
With every turn, a new surprise.
Chasing clouds and dodging bees,
Life's a game of hide-and-seek!

Maps are merely fancy scrolls,
Leading us to endless goals.
Yet every wrong turn we take,
Brings a laugh, a cheer, a break!

So let's rejoice when we are led,
To twisty paths and crumbs of bread.
For in the fluke of every roam,
We may just find our way back home.

Lost Maps and Hidden Paths

View the world through skewed lenses,
Where 'X' marks the spot of fences.
Maps are mere suggestions there,
Adventure waits beyond despair.

Taking wrong roads, what a treat,
Snack on donuts, not just wheat.
Each detour is a brand new game,
With treasure hunts, we stake our claim.

Winding paths are more than guides,
They keep our hearts in wild rides.
Find a dog who steals your shoe,
And laughs at how you don't know too.

So follow whims, embrace the weird,
In goofy turns, be not aird.
For in each twist and silly fling,
We stitch a tale, we dance, we sing!

Invisible trails are the best art,
Painting memories upon the heart.
Lose the map and let it go,
In crooked paths, the joy will flow!

The Art of Wandering

If a path seems worn and dull,
Step aside, just give a pull.
Find the trail that looks absurd,
Follow it, you may disturb!

Invisible signs that nudge us near,
To frolic with a wandering deer.
Each curve brings a chuckle, a grin,
What's lost can be found with a spin!

Collect the moments like bright stones,
In pockets full of rambunctious tones.
Trip on roots, roll in the dew,
Let the wild child inside break through!

A detour is a secret door,
To tales yet written, and so much more.
So sprinkle joy on every street,
And make the ordinary feel complete.

With every misstep and silly dare,
You'll find laughter floating in air.
It's not about where you arrive,
But the giggles you collect, to thrive!

Embracing the Unexpected Turns

Around the bend, a splash of mud,
Dancing shoes? What a dud!
But in the gunk of sudden spills,
Are stories rich with quirky thrills.

Who knew a puddle could make you slip,
And send you off on a goofy trip?
With every turn, a tale unfurls,
As laughter bounces, twirls and whirls.

Traffic lights that turn to disco,
We're stuck here, but watch us go!
Every delay a moment rare,
A chance to laugh, to stop, to stare.

Some will chart their linear course,
Missing joy with every source.
But we, the tricksters, snicker loud,
Take every curve and wear it proud!

So here's to bumps and bouncy rides,
With every twist, our inner child glides.
Embrace the chaos, join the fun,
For in the mess, the magic's spun!

The Dance of the Wayward Traveler

With a map that's upside down, oh what a sight,
I took the wrong turn, what a delightful fright.
The GPS is singing a siren's song,
But I twirl with the uncertain, it won't be long.

A cow looks at me, like "Where's your head?"
I follow squirrels and my own silly thread.
I tried a shortcut, it's become a dead end,
But I'm laughing and giggling, just me and my pretend.

Each twist and turn, brings laughter so bright,
A chocolate fountain in the moon's soft light.
Forget the roadmap, it's never quite right,
Just dance through the chaos, the stars shining white.

So here's to the wanderers, on paths so bizarre,
With shoes that get muddy, and dreams that go far.
For in every wrong turn, there's a laugh to be found,
And a treasure may fall, from a tree on the ground.

Embracing the Nexus of Now

Stop! In the middle of the crossroad I freeze,
Which way should I go? Time tends to tease.
A chicken runs by; I'm caught in a jest,
Is it dinner or life? I'll just let fate rest.

Oh, how I ponder on paths and their bends,
When the ice cream truck comes, all worries it mends.
I'll buy some sprinkles and a big ol' cone,
Perhaps I'll just stay here, forever alone.

The clouds above giggle, as they twist and they turn,
With every bad choice, I just have to learn.
A dance with a cactus, a jog with sheer glee,
Embracing the moment, just wild and free!

So here's to the now, the quirky and bright,
With unexpected chaos, it's a joyful flight.
May our adventures be peppered with laughter loud,
As we wade through the odd, feeling oh-so-proud.

Twilight Trails of Thought

Underneath the stars, my thoughts start to roam,
With a sock on my foot, I forgot to go home.
I follow my shadow down the curious street,
Where the cats throw confetti, and all creatures greet.

The air tastes like lemonade, sweet and so bright,
As I trip over dreams in the soft, silver light.
A flash of a memory, lost like a purse,
Then bubbles erupt, oh what a fun curse!

Each corner brings giggles, strangers throw cheer,
They dance with their worries, with nothing to fear.
Eccentric delights in the twilight so grand,
As I wander these trails of my own whimsical land.

So if you find nonsense is tickling the tree,
Just join in the antics, come share it with me.
For a journey of laughs is the grandest of dreams,
In the twilight of thought, where nothing's as it seems.

Overlooked Wonders in the Journey

I tripped over daisies, a laugh in the sun,
"Remember the path!" but oh, this is fun!
My phone takes a picture of dirt on my nose,
But nature is laughing at all of the prose.

An owl hoots a riddle; I ponder, I'm stuck,
My lunch runs away, oh what rotten luck!
With sandwiches giddy, they fly through the air,
While ants grab my crumbs, without any care.

I'm sailing with puddles, my shoes full of glee,
Like boats in the ocean, wild and carefree.
An umbrella finds shelter for squirrels on parade,
Oh, the wonders I find, all the whims I've parlayed!

The world is a canvas, a laughing delight,
With blunders and stumbles that feel just right.
So raise a fine toast, to the sights and the sounds,
For magic is woven in the chaos we've found.

Discoveries in the Forgotten Nooks

In corners where the dust collects,
There's treasure hiding, who detects?
A sock that once had company,
And crumbs from last week's bakery spree.

A question mark under the old chair,
Labeled "Life's to-do"—but who would care?
Forgotten naps on ancient floors,
A mystery called 'Who closed those doors?'

Old shoes with stories yet untold,
Worn thin like the budget of gold.
Each step a giggle, a chance to roam,
Finding joys in each hidden home.

Like letters lost, but oh so sweet,
In every crack, a funny defeat.
For in each crevice lies a light,
That turns our fumbles into flight.

The Tapestry of Wanderlust

With maps that twist like curly fries,
Each turn unveils a new surprise.
A wrong way leads to ice cream shops,
Where every scoop is laughter that pops.

We search the skies and trudge the ground,
In search of wonders yet unfound.
A burrito spill on a road-trip snack,
Turns 'let's find food' into 'get the nap!'

Bright neon signs that catch the eye,
Offer tacos or a pie to try.
With each fork spilled, we learn to grin,
As laughter finds its way back in.

For every bump and twisty track,
Is fuel for tales, no holding back.
We weave wild dreams, both hot and cold,
In bowls of chaos, our lives unfold.

When Wander Takes the Lead

Maps are for people with no sense of play,
We'll follow the frogs, they'll show us the way.
Through puddles and mud, we leap like pros,
Chasing butterflies, we forget our woes.

On a path that's not paved, we meet a goat,
Wearing a crown made of plastic, what a quote!
We laugh at the road signs, upside-down and wild,
Every turn welcomes our inner child.

With snacks that tumble and drinks that spill,
Each hiccup we share is an added thrill.
As wander leads us on a merry chase,
We find joy in the scenery's silly face.

So here's to the joy of uncharted plans,
Where laughter is currency, and fun reigns sans.
Together we travel, with hearts that are free,
For wandering kinds are just meant to be.

Adventures Found in Bumps and Bruises

With every trip there's a slip and slide,
We fall for the splendors we can't abide.
That tumble down the hill, a comedy of errors,
Turns giggles to clouds, with life's little terrors.

A bruised knee from trying to dance,
Bumping into a fence, just chance on chance.
But oh, those giggles, they make us feel light,
In every misstep, there's pure delight.

From wandering pathways where wildflowers bloom,
To tripping on roots, we embrace the gloom.
Every bruise tells a story we wear with pride,
Insanity's passport, a joyful ride.

So take all the bumps with a wink and a smile,
For the best of adventures go on for a mile.
Embrace every tumble, let laughter ensue,
With scars as our badges, we'll wander anew.

Tales of the Unexpected Route

I planned to take the highway fast,
But ended up in a field with cows.
The GPS lost signal, oh what a blast,
Now I'm an expert at herding sows.

I thought I'd grab a quick bite to eat,
Ended up at a llama petting zoo.
Llamas with carrots were quite the treat,
But I might need a shower, it's true.

My road trip snacks turned into a feast,
Disguised as gourmet at a roadside stand.
I'm pretty sure I saw a feral beast,
But it was just a raccoon, all unplanned.

But here's to roads that twist and turn,
Where every wrong turn brings some cheer.
Each silly moment is what we earn,
And laughter is the best souvenir.

Footprints on the Wayward Trail.

Out for a jog, I took a left,
Thought it would lead to the coffee shop.
But instead, I found a treasure chest,
Filled with socks and a single mop.

The trees started talking, oh what a sight,
Asking for help with their tangled roots.
I tried to reason, but how could I fight?
They said, 'Just wait 'til we sprout some boots.'

Chasing squirrels, I lost my way,
Stumbled upon a party of ants.
They had more fun than I did that day,
Dancing in circles, I joined their chants.

So here's to trails that go astray,
Where giggles bloom and frowns fall flat.
In every misstep, there's joy at play,
And stories to share, how 'bout that?

Winding Roads of Tomorrow

On the map, it looked like a straight line,
But GPS led me through a goat farm.
I ended up sipping goat's milk fine,
While they debated if math could be charm.

Each twist and turn brings a funny sight,
A yard sale bumper cars, oh what a thrill!
I never knew a dancing cat could bite,
Until it jumped out to make a deal.

Chickens auditioning for a cooking show,
Strutting around like they own the place.
I waved at a llama, "Let's take it slow!"
Chasing dreams at a plodding pace.

So cheers to roads that refuse to end,
Where laughter sticks and worries dissolve.
With friends on the way, it's hearts we mend,
And more funny stories to evolve.

The Scenic Route to Nowhere

I decided to take the scenic route,
Finding paths less traveled and wide.
Met a duck who thought he was astute,
Claiming he'd be my trusty guide.

He led me to a lake of soap bubbles,
Where fish wore hats and danced in a line.
I tried to join, but my feet had troubles,
With slippery shoes, I fell—oh, what a sign!

My snacks turned into a picnic for ants,
As they petitioned for a better deal.
In exchange for crumbs, they'd share their plans,
Of making a dance that would seal the meal.

So here on this route with uproarious glee,
Misadventures blossom like flowers in spring.
Each twist and turn sings along with the bee,
For the journey's a joke and joy is the king.

www.ingramcontent.com/pod-product-compliance
Lightning Source LLC
Chambersburg PA
CBHW051659160426
43209CB00004B/955